To our children,
Eloise, Greta, and Simon –
We love every cell of you
with all of our hearts.
Love,
Mom and Dad

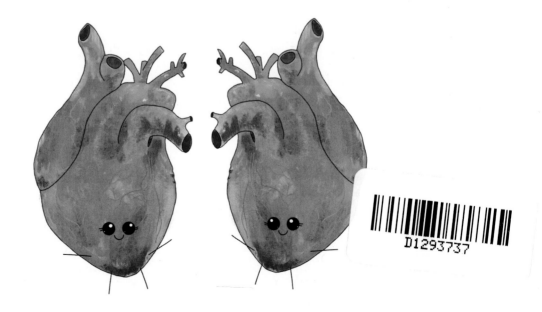

Table of Contents

* We are in alignment with the American Medical Association's policy Medical Spectrum of Gender D-295.3 12, which "affirms that an individual's genotypic sex, phenotypic sex, sexual orientation, gender and gender identity are not always aligned or indicative of the other, and that gender for many individuals may differ from the sex assigned at birth." The terms female and male are used in this book to describe organs typically associated with the sex assigned at birth, though we honor the continuum and complexity of sex, gender, and gender identity.

Introduction

This silly book of poems
Is really quite complete.
We talk about the organs
From the head down to the feet.

We do want you to know
That the body's quite complex.
If we wrote about each cell,
You'd be reading 'til Sunday next.

While this book is surely goofy,
We hope that you discern,
What's meant to make you laugh
And what's meant to help you learn.

Like organs don't have faces,
But we thought it made them cute.
If you know learning should be fun,
You must be quite astute.

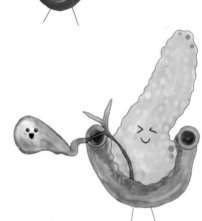

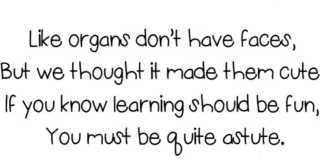

Big Beautiful Brain

(To the tune of "Twinkle Twinkle Little Star")

Thinking thinking gorgeous brain
You manage
My thoughts,
My feelings,
My pain.

You control the systems in my body
Like when
To eat,
To sleep,
To potty.

Thinking thinking gorgeous brain
You're protected by three membranes.

2

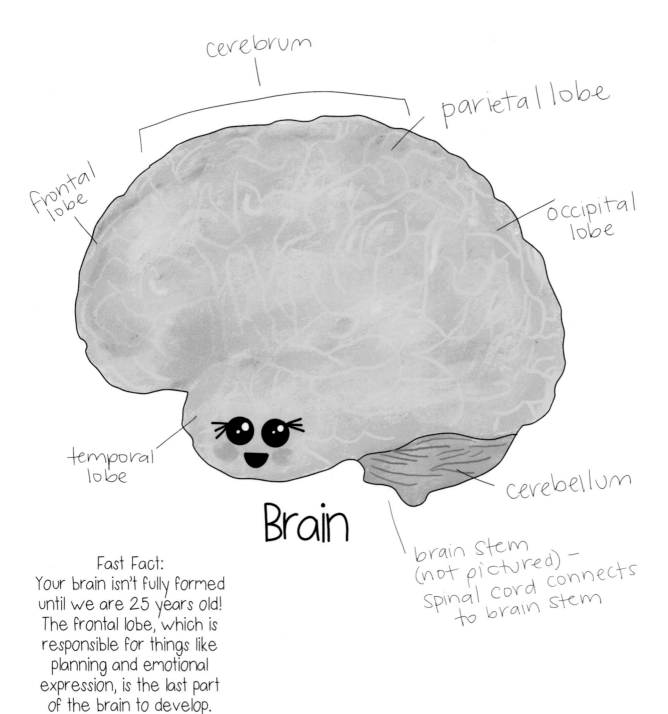

cerebrum

parietal lobe

frontal lobe

occipital lobe

temporal lobe

cerebellum

Brain

brain stem
(not pictured) –
spinal cord connects
to brain stem

Fast Fact:
Your brain isn't fully formed
until we are 25 years old!
The frontal lobe, which is
responsible for things like
planning and emotional
expression, is the last part
of the brain to develop.

3

Eye See You

Eye love me
Eye help you see
Eye think some things we can agree
Eye am complex

Eye'm most commonly brown
Eye won't let you sneeze while looking around
Eye'm made of two million different parts and
Eye've been known to break some hearts.
Eye have a cornea to help me focus
and a pupil to let light in.

Eye have an iris, that's the colorful part, made up from melanin.
Eye'm mostly hiding back in your head, there's a lot you cannot see.
In fact, the outside parts you see are just one sixth of me.

4

Fast Fact:
The average person blinks around 12 times a minute.

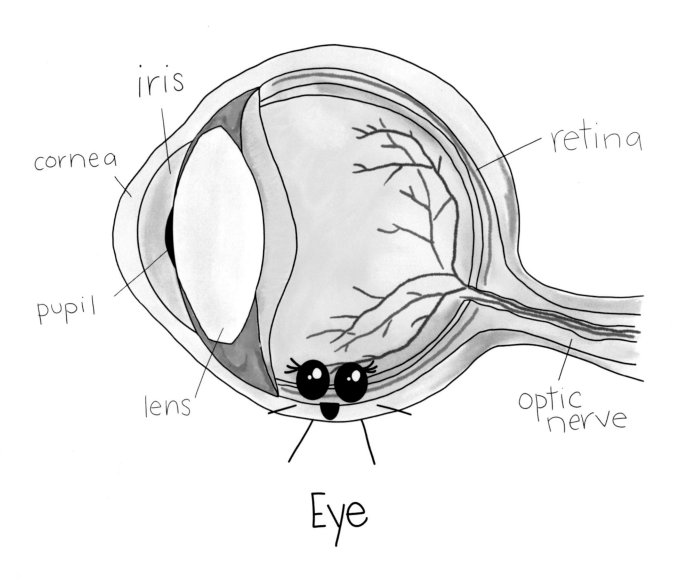

iris

cornea

retina

pupil

lens

optic
nerve

Eye

Strike a (Spinal) Cord

I'm a tube-like band of tissues
From your back up to your brain.
I make sure there are no issues
With feeling pressure, touch, or pain.

Electrical messages travel down the spine,
And from there out to the nerves.
Where the messages are passed along
To the body parts they serve.

Fast Fact:
Your spinal cord stops growing around the age of 4
(up to 16-20 inches long), but after that it doesn't
grow any longer! (The vertebral column, also known
as the spine or the backbone, continues to grow
around the spinal cord well into the teenage years).

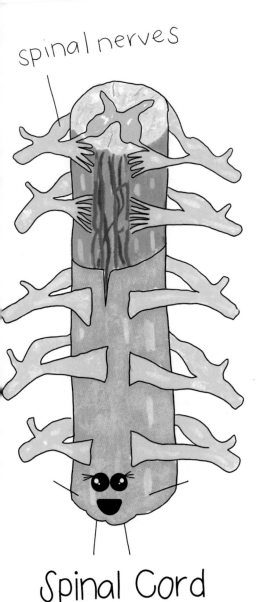

spinal nerves

Spinal Cord

Think of me as a highway,
And the nerves as smaller streets.
The electrical currents are messages
Being delivered by a fleet

Of cars that are on that highway,
Turning off on smaller roads
Delivering the messages
Just where they need to go.

When it's time to take a walk,
Your brain lets your body know
By sending electrical currents
From your head down to your toes.

A Sonnet from the Heart

Let's get to the heart of the matter,
The body really admires my beat.
My rhythm is not just for chatter,
It pumps blood down to your feet.

Blood travels through two different systems,
Arteries and veins, red and blue.
Veins bring blood to the heart
Arteries take blood to the rest of you.

I've got four chambers, they're kind of like rooms
Atrium and ventricle, left and right.
My walls squeeze blood so it zooms
All through the body day and night.

My valves are like doors,
They let blood flow through
So I get the job done
And you can be you.

8

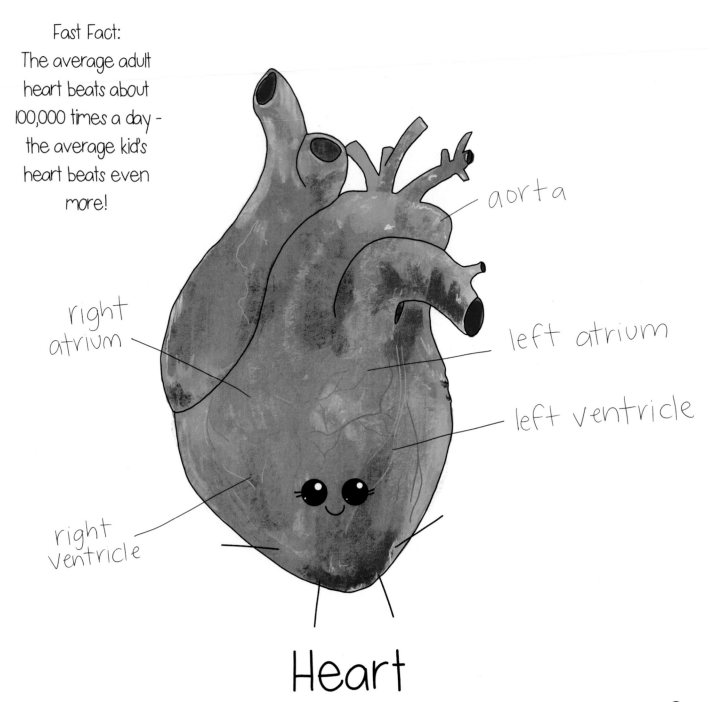

aorta

right atrium

left atrium

left ventricle

right ventricle

Heart

9

Say Ahhh

Open wide and look way back
In your throat and you will see
On each side there is a tonsil -
They help with immunity.

We used to think they didn't do much,
But we know now that's not true
They keep you healthy by keeping out junk,
And make antibodies too.

Fast Fact:
There are actually four different kinds of
tonsils, but the ones that we usually talk
about (and the ones referred to in this
book) are called the palatine tonsils.

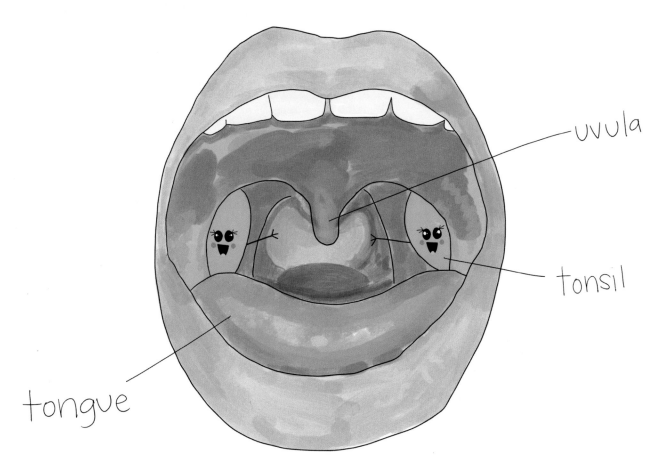

uvula

tonsil

tongue

Tonsils

Speaking of the Larynx

I'm the voice box, called the larynx,
I house the vocal cords so you can speak.
A tube that connects to the pharynx,
Without me, air would leak.

You breathe in air with your mouth and nose,
To the pharynx (or throat as it is known),
Then down my tube air only flows,
This is a no-food zone.

The larger I am, the deeper you'll sound,
If I'm small, you may be squeaking.
If I am inflamed all around,
You may not do much speaking.

12

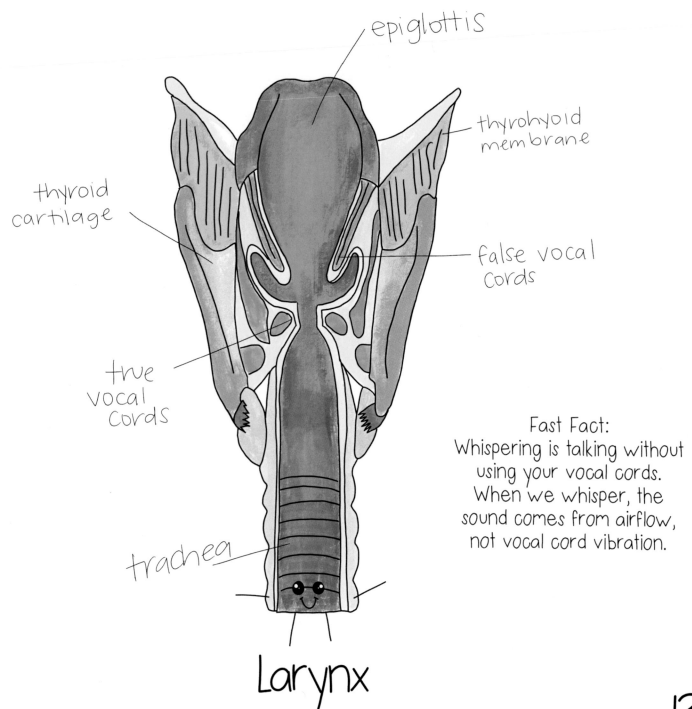

epiglottis

thyrohyoid membrane

thyroid cartilage

false vocal cords

true vocal cords

Fast Fact:
Whispering is talking without using your vocal cords. When we whisper, the sound comes from airflow, not vocal cord vibration.

trachea

Larynx

13

Take My Breath Away

The trachea, the wind pipe.
It helps us to get air.
It certainly lives up to the hype –
Of this, you are aware.

Larynx
To the
Pharynx
To the
Trachea,
Which splits in two.

These are called the bronchi,
The air just flows right through.
It flows right through into each lung...
And that must mean this poem is done.

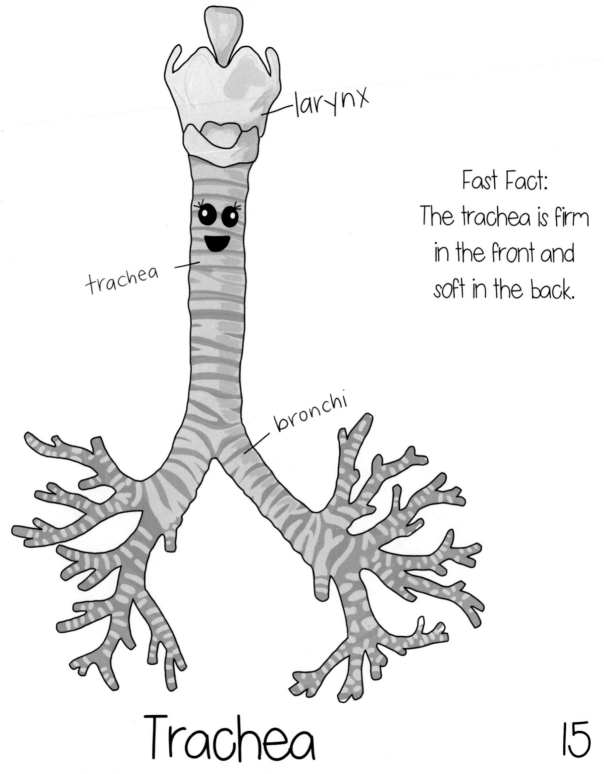

larynx

trachea

bronchi

Fast Fact:
The trachea is firm
in the front and
soft in the back.

Trachea

Fresh Air

Lungs, you're an important part of my body,
You always keep it fresh.
By 'it' of course, I mean the air I breathe,
You keep me in the flesh.
The air is made of several gasses,
We need oxygen the most.
When I breathe it in,
You move the oxygen,
And the blood becomes its host.
The blood takes the oxygen to the rest of the body,
Where it's traded for CO
That garbage gas gets sent back to the lungs
Then you breathe out that trash, woohoo!

16

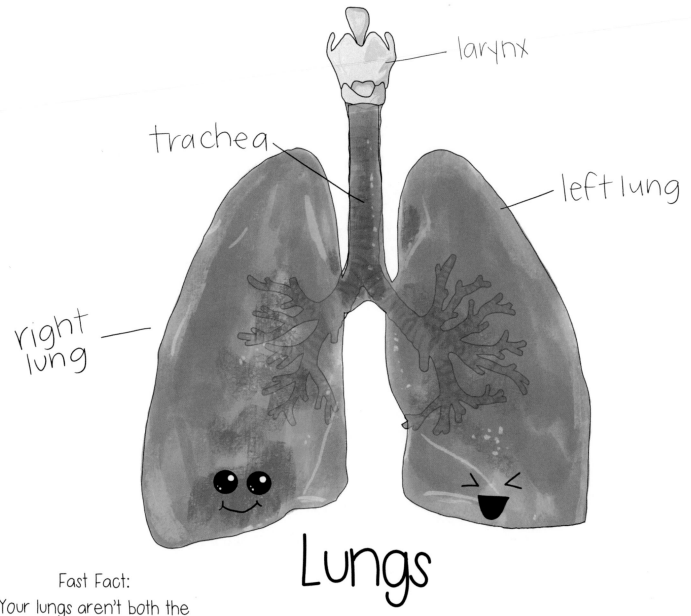

larynx

trachea

left lung

right lung

Lungs

Fast Fact:
Your lungs aren't both the same size - the right lung is larger than the left lung to make room for the heart.

Not Hard to Swallow

Apples, peaches, pumpkin pie,
Water, juice, or tea.
Food and drink start in your mouth,
And then they come to me.
A hollow tube from mouth to tummy,
I'm kind of like a slide.
Once you chew and swallow your food,
It goes on quite a ride.
When food is down inside of me,
I start to do the wave.
My muscles squeeze the food down further,
That motion's what I crave.
Once the food has reached the stomach,
I've done my job all right.
I drop it off and gear back up —
You're taking your next bite!

18

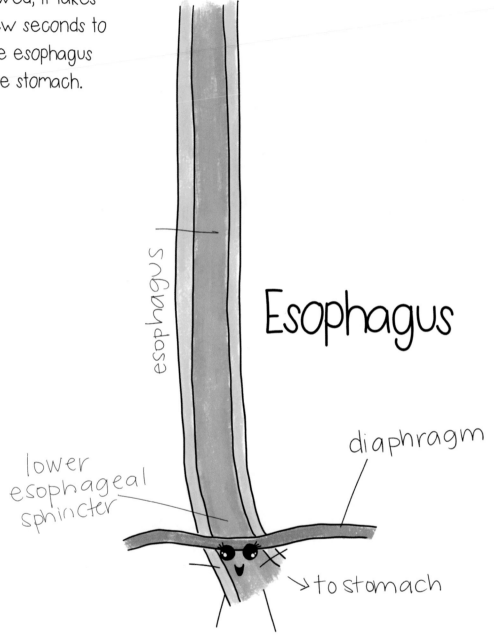

Fast Fact:
Once swallowed, it takes
food only a few seconds to
go down the esophagus
and into the stomach.

esophagus

Esophagus

diaphragm

lower
esophageal
sphincter

→ to stomach

19

Digest This

Sphincters seal the stomach,
They relax to let food in.
The stomach seeps secretions,
Enzymes break down lunch and din.

Muscles move and mix the meal,
Stomach stores food like an inn.
After a while it's check out time,
Next stop: the small intestine.

Fast Fact:
Digestion doesn't actually begin in the stomach - it starts in the mouth. When you chew, saliva (also known as spit) mixes with the food and starts to break it down a little.

esophagus

duodenum

Stomach

It Takes Guts

The intestines are a system,
And they're really quite complex.
Let's explore the different parts,
And all of their effects.

The stomach is where they start,
And they end up at the anus.
They're really very long,
Like a red carpet when you're famous.

The small intestine is actually quite long,
 20 feet to be exact.
It's about an inch in diameter,
It really is well-packed.

The large intestine is 5 feet long,
So it's shorter than the small,
At 3 inches in diameter,
It's wide, but it's not tall.

Food goes from the stomach to the small intestine,
It takes from what you eat.
It sucks out all the vitamins,
It's really very neat.

Food then flows over to the large intestine,
Also called the colon.
It takes the water out of the food,
The digestive tract is rollin'!

Food without its nutrients
Becomes a different group,
Because once it's in the colon,
It's now considered poop.

The intestines have taken what they need
To keep the body great.
The poop heads to the rectum next,
Now it's time to defecate.

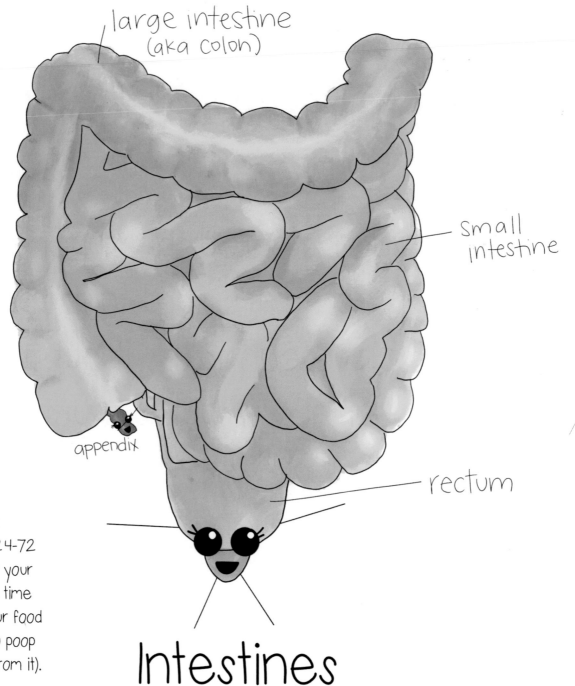

large intestine
(aka colon)

small
intestine

rectum

appendix

Fun Fact:
It takes about 24-72
hours to digest your
food (from the time
you swallow your food
to the time you poop
out the waste from it).

Intestines

23

Mysterious Appendix

This organ is called the appendix
When infected, it's hard to mend it.
The surgeon takes it out,
You'll live, without a doubt.
Though you may wish that you could
befriend it.

24

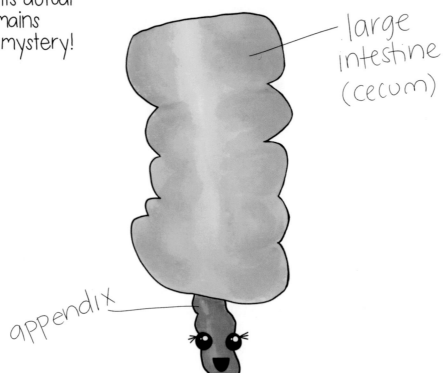

large intestine (cecum)

appendix

Appendix

A Poem that de-Livers

The liver is quite a big deal,
With over 500 important jobs.
Like cleaning out toxins from the blood,
Blood cells can be quite the slobs.

It also makes bile for other organs,
To help the intestines digest.
It stores vitamins and minerals —
Aren't you so impressed?

But that's not all, there's so much more
About the liver to adore:

It's the largest solid organ,
3-ish pounds, that dark red liver.
It takes out sugar from the blood,
This organ sure delivers.

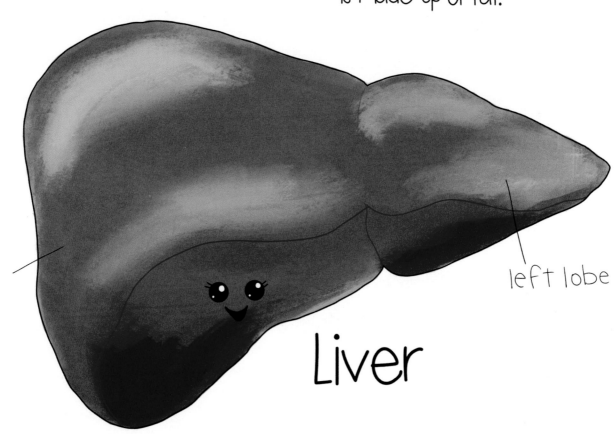

Fast Fact:
10% of our liver
is made up of fat.

right
lobe

left lobe

Liver

27

Sweet, Sweet Pancreas

The pancreas creates natural juices
Used to break down food.
These juices, which are called enzymes,
Go to the small intestine once brewed.

This part is called the exocrine function,
Because it helps you digest,
All the food you ate at luncheon,
To make you your very best.

The pancreas also has an endocrine function,
Which really is quite neat.
It releases hormones to the blood,
So you don't get too sweet.

Fast Fact:
The pancreas has taste buds (similar to those on the tongue) to "taste" sweetness in the blood (and then send out the appropriate amount of insulin to balance out the blood sugar).

pancreas

duodenum
(small intestine)

Pancreas

Won't You Stay a Bile?

gallbladder

left hepatic duct

right hepatic duct

cystic duct

common bile duct

If you need to store some bile
(the stuff that breaks down fat)
No need to look a while
The gallbladder's there for that!
It sits just under your liver
And is part of the digestive system
While you eat, it squeezes to deliver
The bile to your small intestine.

Fast Fact:
You can live
without your
gallbladder, and the
surgery to remove
it is called a
cholecystectomy.

I Can Ex-Spleen It

There once was an organ named Spleen,
It's job is to get blood so clean.
It fights your infections
And stays in its section
Right under the rib cage, serene.

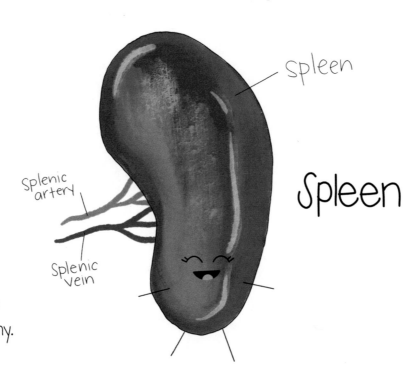

spleen

Splenic artery

Splenic vein

Spleen

Fun Fact:
It's possible to live without your spleen - the surgery to remove it is called a splenectomy.

If Urine, You're In

There once was an organ named Bladder.
But why does this thing even matter?
It holds all your pee,
Works with the kidney,
If it leaks, you may feel badder.

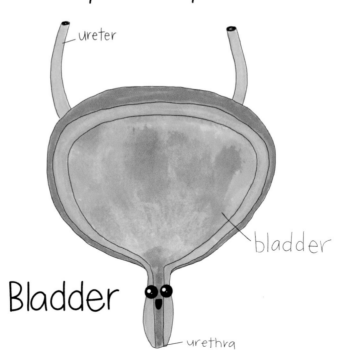

ureter

Bladder

bladder

urethra

Fast Fact:
The average adult bladder can hold about 2 cups (16 ounces) of urine. To know how much a child's bladder can hold, divide their age by 2 (if they're older than 2), then add 6. An 8 year old's bladder can hold about 10 ounces of urine.

Kidneys, Not Kid Knees

(To the tune of "Row, Row, Row Your Boat")

The kidneys do a lot
To keep your body clean
They remove toxins and extra water
And use it to make pee.

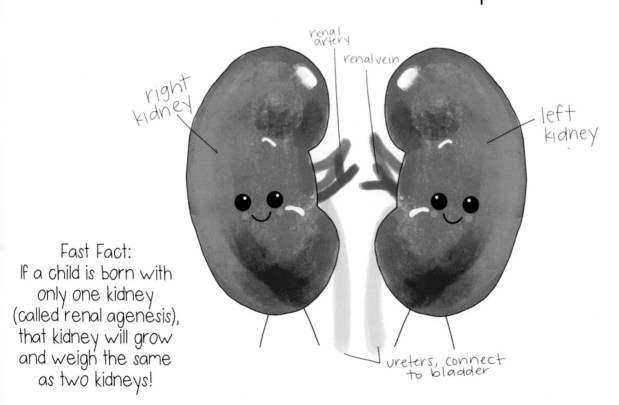

renal artery

renal vein

right kidney

left kidney

Fast Fact:
If a child is born with only one kidney (called renal agenesis), that kidney will grow and weigh the same as two kidneys!

ureters, connect to bladder

33

Breast Poem Ever

The breasts are the organs right on the chest
Everyone's born with them, yes it's true.
We start out with nipples and as we grow up,
Females' breasts start growing up too.

For most males they have no function
(Unless you're a masked fox or fruit bat)
For females they do a few things,
And get their shape during puberty from fat.

Female breasts have a special kind of tissue
That can make milk if there is a need.
The milk travels down tiny tubes called ducts
And then out the nipple in order to feed.

The nipple is the bump in the middle of the breast,
The areola is the dark circle surrounding
Every breast looks different in shape color and size
Isn't the thought of that just astounding?

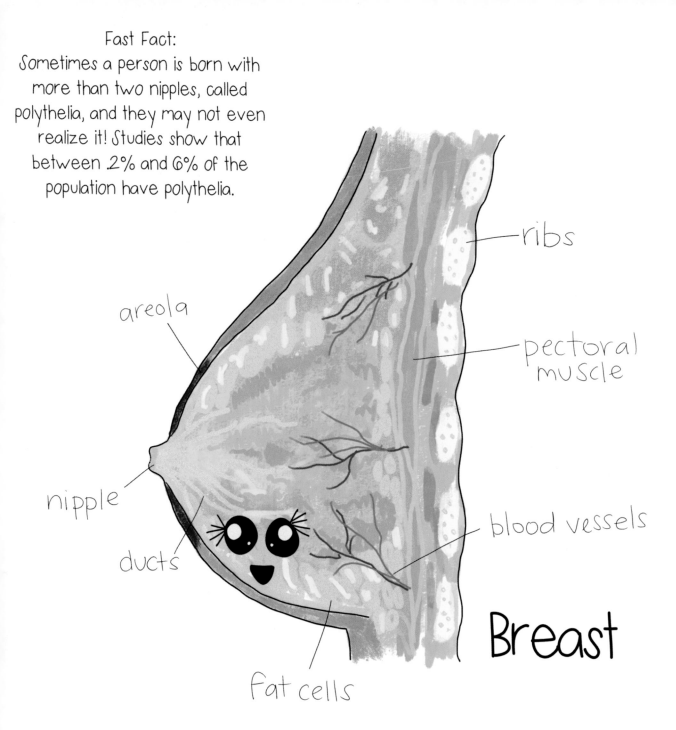

Fast Fact:
Sometimes a person is born with more than two nipples, called polythelia, and they may not even realize it! Studies show that between .2% and 6% of the population have polythelia.

ribs

areola

pectoral muscle

nipple

ducts

blood vessels

fat cells

Breast

35

Urethra, We've Got It!

The birds and the bees
have nothing on me,
The penis and the scrotum
and of course, the testes.

The scrotum is the sack that holds the testes,
Its job is to keep them safe.
Too warm and it drops low, too cool it pulls up,
Sometimes movement makes it chafe.

Sperm is the seed used to make babies,
It travels down the vas deferens.
From there it goes out the end of the penis,
And my role in baby making ends.

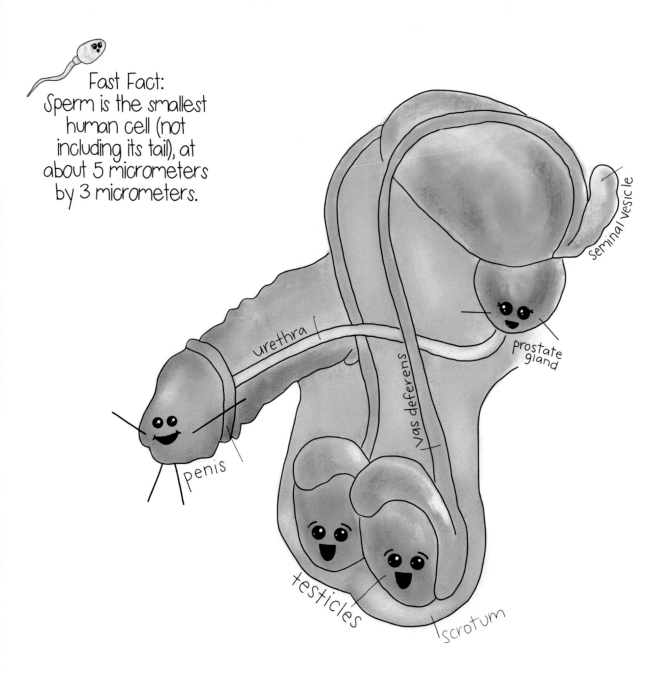

Fast Fact:
Sperm is the smallest human cell (not including its tail), at about 5 micrometers by 3 micrometers.

seminal vesicle

prostate gland

urethra

vas deferens

penis

testicles

scrotum

Male Reproductive System

37

At Your Cervix

It takes three key things to make a baby,
(Though that's not all I do).
The male reproductive has one of those things,
I have the other two.

The sperm (key part one) is like a seed,
It comes straight from the male.
It needs to meet an egg (key part two)
To begin this baby tale.

Eggs are stored in my ovaries,
Every month one gets released.
It travels to my uterus (key part three!)
Where it is then unleashed.

If sperm enters my uterus
While an egg is on its way
They meet up in the fallopian tube
To share some DNA.

The egg and sperm together,
Now combined and called a zygote,
Travels down the tube to the uterine wall,
40 weeks it will devote,

To dividing and dividing and dividing some more
Blastocyte > Embryo > Fetus.
Nine months later a baby comes out
And if you don't believe us

Go look in the mirror at your perfect self,
From your head down to your toes,
You once started as an egg and sperm
Which now, of course, you know.

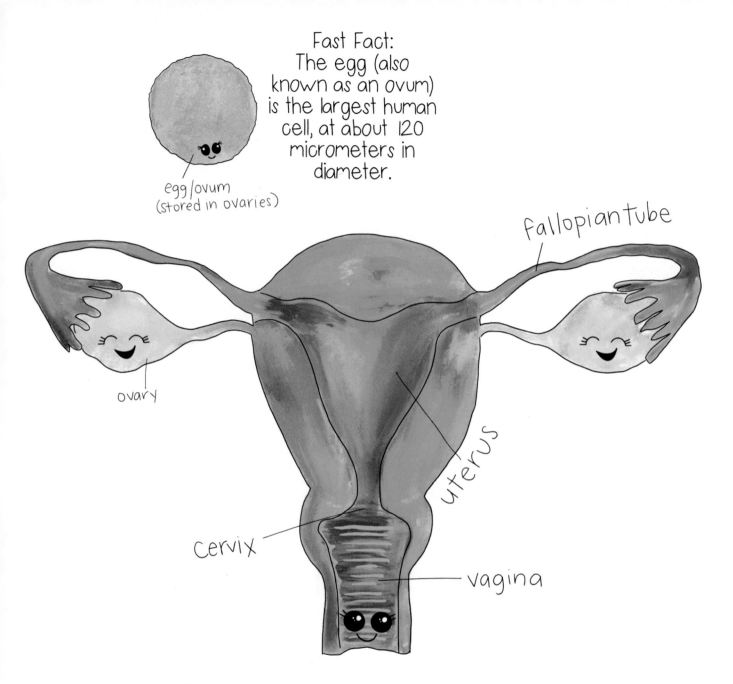

Fast Fact:
The egg (also known as an ovum) is the largest human cell, at about 120 micrometers in diameter.

egg/ovum
(stored in ovaries)

fallopian tube

ovary

uterus

cervix

vagina

Female Reproductive System

Skin - That's a Wrap
(Best read out loud with someone nearby beatboxing)

I'm the skin, the skin,
I hold the organs in.
The epidermis   'Missssss
The hypodermis   'Missssss
The plain old dermis   'Missssss
Without me you would be amiss 'Missssss

Melanin gives me my color
The world would be a whole lot duller
Without it, we'd all look the same
No offense other organs,
But that's lame.

40

Fast Fact:
It's normal for us to lose skin cells - in other words, for the epidermis (the layer of skin we can see from the outside) to flake off. In fact, we lose about 30,000-40,000 dead skin cells per minute! That's almost 9 pounds of skin cells per year (about how much the average cat weighs).

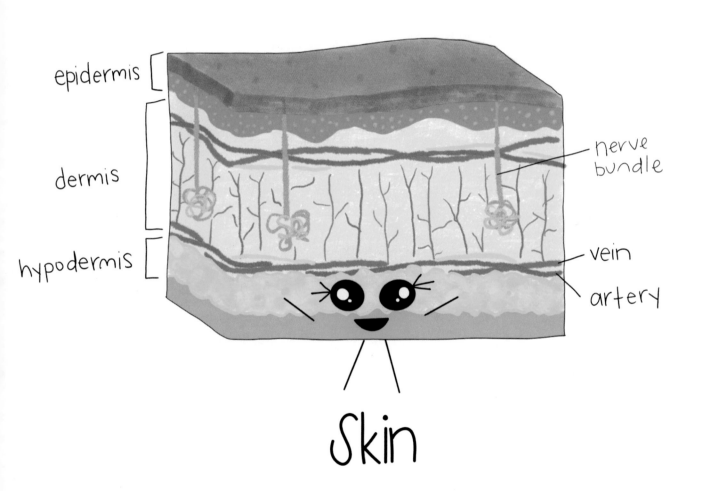

epidermis

dermis

hypodermis

nerve bundle

vein

artery

Skin

Everyday I'm Muscle'n

The muscles allow us to speak and chew,
They control the heartbeat and breathing too.

With over 600 from head to toe,
Muscles have quite the portfolio.

There are three different types that you should know-
Cardiac, smooth, and skeletal.

The gluteus maximus is the largest one -
The muscle also known as your bum!

Fast Fact:
The smallest muscles in your
body are in your inner ear
(that's also where the
smallest bones are!)

(connects to the bone)

tendon

muscle
fiber

Funny Bones

The bones in the body
Have some mighty jobs,
Without them
We would all be blobs.

We'd have no shape,
No chance of standing.
Just puddles of people,
Slowly expanding.

They're living tissue,
They offer protection,
To keep the organs
In states of perfection.

We're born with 300,
And as we grow,
The number begins to go down low.
The bones connect,
They start to mix,
Until we have 206.

Fast Fact:
The thigh bone
(called the femur) is
the longest and
strongest bone in
the human body.

Hormoneous Thyroid

I'm shaped quite like a butterfly,
Though I won't fly away.
You'll find me at the front of the neck,
And this is where I'll stay.

I'm called a gland, which simply means,
I release things called hormones.
Those are chemicals with messages,
Like I'm playing Telephone.

I help the body function,
I help the body grow,
I help maintain its temperature,
Not too high and not too low.

Fast Fact:
A healthy thyroid is just a little bigger than a quarter.

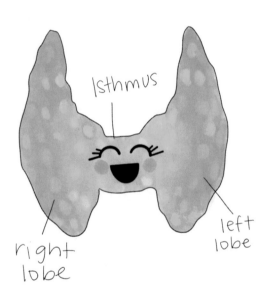

Isthmus

right lobe

left lobe

Gland to Meet You

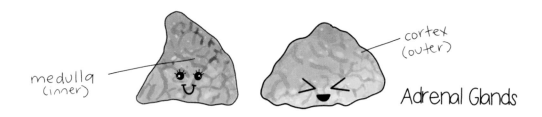

medulla (inner)

cortex (outer)

Adrenal Glands

The adrenal glands, shaped like ice cream cones,
Sit right atop the kidneys.
They release hormones that that are super important -
They're vital, if you please.

Each gland has two parts,
The outer and inner.
The cortex and medulla,
For any adrenal beginners.

The cortex releases cortisol,
A hormone with lots of urgency.
It impacts your sleep and wake cycles,
And boosts energy during emergencies.

The second part, the Medulla,
I wonder if you could guess,
That it releases a hormone called adrenaline,
Which helps you during stress.

Map of the Body
(not to scale)

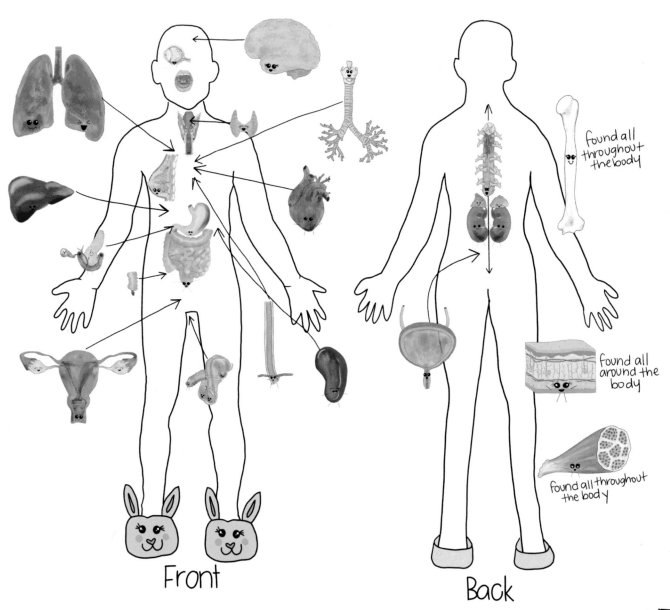

found all throughout the body

found all around the body

found all throughout the body

Front

Back

Glossary

Antibodies

Antibodies are things made from part of the blood (called plasma) that helps to fight germs and infection so you don't get sick.

Arteries

Arteries are tubes of blood that carry oxygen away from your heart and into your body.

Cells

Cells are the smallest living unit that make up all living things. Imagine your body was made of Legos; each Lego is like a cell. Together, the Legos join to make a building or a tower just like the cells join to make you! A cell has three main parts - the membrane, the nucleus, and the cytoplasm. Different cells have different jobs, to build different parts of the body.

Chemicals

The world is made up of different things, or substances, called chemicals. Hormones are a specific type of chemical in your body that make your organs do certain things. For example, insulin is one hormone that makes sure you have the right amount of sugar in your blood.

Diameter

A diameter is the measurement from one side of a circle to the other side, straight through the middle.

Digest

To digest is to break down the food you eat into smaller parts, so the body can absorb and use the nutrients.

Defecate

Defecate is a fancy way of saying to poop.

Duct

A duct is like a small tube or passageway that things travel through (in the body, these things are often hormones). For example, most homes have heating ducts for heated air to go through to heat up the house.

Endocrine

Endocrine glands send out hormones without ducts, directly into the bloodstream.

Enzymes

Something called a protein that helps a change take place within the body (also known as a chemical reaction). The enzymes in the stomach, for example, helps to digest food.

Exocrine

Exocrine glands send out products through ducts.

Gasses

There are three types of things - solids (like the couch or chair you're sitting), liquids (like water you drink), and gasses (like steam that rises when food cooks). Just like there can be different types of solids (crayons, this book, a blanket) and liquids (water, juice, milk), there are different types of gasses (like the gas helium, used to fill up balloons and make them float, is different than when you use your breath, also a gas, to blow up balloons). When you see steam rising from a pot of boiling water, that gas is water vapor.

Glands

Glands are a type of organ in your body, and they usually make something and release it (like sweat glands in the skin release sweat, the mammary glands in the breast make milk to feed a baby).

Hormones

Hormones are the body's chemical messengers, sending messages to different parts of the body to do different things. For example, during puberty (see below), your body releases different hormones (than when you were younger) so certain parts of you begin to grow.

Infection

An infection is when germs get into your body and make you sick.

Immune System

The immune system is part of your body that protects you against germs that make you sick. The word "immunity" means how strong your immune system is to protect against a specific sickness.

Membrane

A membrane is a thin layer of cells or tissue that covers an organ, like how your skin covers your body.

Melanin

Melanin is a pigment in the body that gives color to certain things, like the skin and the eyes. Think of it like a watercolor paint - the more you have, the darker your skin and eyes will be. The less you have, the lighter your skin and eyes will be.

Nerves

You have special cells (called neurons) to send different messages to the body. These neurons travel

Organs

A part of the body with specific important functions.

Oxygen

Oxygen is a gas in the air that most living things need to breathe in to live.

Puberty

A time when a person's body becomes sexually mature (meaning the body is able to reproduce, or create a baby). This usually happens between the ages of 10-14 years old.

Sphincter
A circle-shaped muscle that squeezes to keep things in and relaxes to let things through.

Tissues
A tissue is a group of cells that work together to do a specific job. There are four different types of tissue in the human body - muscle tissue, epithelial tissue, connective tissue, and nervous tissue.

Toxins
Another word for poison - things that are bad for us and could make us sick. Some toxins can be found outside of the body (like cleaning products around the house), and some toxins are made by our body (and it needs to get rid of them).

Valves
Valves are like doors, opening to let things in, then closing to keep things in (and keep them from going back out). Valves in the heart open to let blood flow through and control the flow of the blood.

Vitamins
Vitamins are things that people need to grow and be healthy. There are 13 vitamins, including Vitamin A, eight different kinds of B vitamins, C, D, E, and K. We get vitamins mostly from food (like fruits and vegetables), but also from other sources like the sun (vitamin D) or from bacteria in our intestines (vitamin K).

Veins
Veins are tubes that bring blood (needing oxygen) to the heart. Pulmonary veins bring red blood with oxygen to the heart from the lungs.

About the Authors

Drs. Christine and Greg Borst live in beautiful sunny Colorado, with their three kids and two dogs. Christine is a licensed therapist with a PhD in Medical Family Therapy, and a former professor who now runs her own business. Greg is a trauma surgeon by day, and also trauma surgeon by night (lol) and an avid collector of whiskey in between. When he's not operating, Greg's participating in whatever scheme Christine has cooked up (like an organ-themed book of poems for kids). They enjoy hiking, traveling, using double-entendres in front of their children, and spending quiet evenings flipping through Netflix each waiting for the other to make a decision.

Instagram: @christineborstcreativestudio & @whiskey_that.is.neat
www.christineborstcreativestudio.com